I Want YOU to Know...

Written by: Leslie Colburn

Illustrated by: Stella Ernes

No longer two small fireflies,
you have vast rays of light!
The spirit that's within your heart
brings sunshine to the night.
You finally get to spread your wings.
It's time for you to soar.
You're ready for what God has planned.

GO ON!

He's opening the door.

I Want You to Know
© 2023 by Leslie Colburn
Graphics and art by Stella Ernes

Unless otherwise indicated, all Scripture quotations are taken from the Holy Bible, New Living Translation, copyright © 1996, 2004, 2015 by Tyndale House Foundation. Used by permission of Tyndale House Publishers, Carol Stream, Illinois 60188. All rights reserved.

No part of this book may be reproduced in any manner without the express written consent of the publisher, except in the case of brief excerpts in reviews and articles. All inquiries should be addressed to:

Cross My Heart Books
www.lesliecolburn.com
lesliecolburnbooks@hotmail.com

Printed in the United States of America
First edition
ISBN 979-8-218-09170-5

Dear   ,

You are growing up so quickly! Do you know everything you need to know? Probably not, but you will learn and grow as you take off on your next adventure. Here are some words of wisdom and reminders to take with you wherever you go.

Believe in yourself because you were created on purpose for a purpose. You are a masterpiece, a piece of the Master. So go and let your light shine!

Most importantly, I want you to know:

GOD LOVES YOU!

Love always,

FAITH

Invite God into your decisions.
Ask Him to guide your feet.
Pray.
Then thank Him for His blessings.

Don't worry about anything; instead, pray about everything; TELL GOD WHAT YOU NEED, and thank Him for all He has done. Then you will experience God's peace, which exceeds anything we can understand. HIS PEACE WILL GUARD YOUR HEARTS and minds as you live in CHRIST JESUS.

PHILIPPIANS 4:6-7 NLT

SEASONS

There are different seasons in life.
Respect where others are in their lives.
Honor where you are in yours.
Seize the day and make it count!

This is the day the Lord has made. WE WILL REJOICE and be glad in it. PSALMS 118:24 NLT

ADVENTURE

Travel and make a difference in the world.

Let people make a difference in you.

Never stop learning.

Watch sunrises and sunsets.

Always use the buddy system.

Call and come home often.

Therefore, go

and make disciples of all nations,

BAPTIZING THEM IN THE NAME

OF THE FATHER AND THE SON

and the Holy Spirit

MATTHEW 28:19 NLT

SELF LOVE

Love the you of the past, the you of today,
and the you of tomorrow.
As you look back at the yous of yesterday,
remember you did your best in that time and
place, so speak words of love to yourself.
Have a little 'me-time' every day.

...LOVES the YOU of tomorrow!
The YOU of the past...

Is it snot or honey?

HEALTH

If it's wet and it's not yours, don't touch it!
(or smell it!)
Move and breathe in the fresh air every day.
Feed your body nutritious food.
Talk about your joys, heartaches, and fears
with someone you trust.
God gave you the ability to laugh and cry;
Do both.

INTEGRITY

Tell the truth. Admit your mistakes.
Leave everyone and everything better
than you found them.
If you drop it, pick it up.
If you get it out, put it away.
If you make a mess...

...clean it up.

Do to others as you would like them TO DO TO YOU.

LUKE 6:31 NLT

YOU MUST EACH DECIDE in your heart how much to give.

AND DON'T GIVE RELUCTANTLY or in response to pressure.

"For God loves a person who gives cheerfully."

2 CORINTHIANS 9:7 NLT

MONEY

Don't spend money you don't have.
Give with a generous and faithful heart.
Save until you have enough to pay cash.
Be self-sufficient.
Everything that you have belongs to God.

GRATITUDE

Notice good things; look for them;
appreciate them.
Accepting a gift blesses you and the
giver.
Write them a thank you note.

Dear Friend,
Thank you so much!
Love always,
Me

PERSEVERANCE

You can do (almost) anything for a year.

TRIALS

When you fall,
you can cry.
You can laugh.
Just get back on your feet.

a time to cry

and a time to laugh.

A TIME TO GRIEVE

and a time to dance

ECCLESIASTES 3:4 NLT

This is my commandment:
LOVE EACH OTHER
IN THE SAME WAY
I have loved you.
JOHN 15:12 NIV

FRIENDSHIPS

Love yourself and others like Jesus does.
In your life, you may only have as many true
friends as you can count on one hand.
Family can be friends. Friends can be family.
Surround yourself with those who build you up,
help you up, encourage you to be your best, and
love like Jesus.

PURPOSE

Whatever you do, do it to the best of your ability.

It's okay to ask for help.

Aim to exceed expectations.

Make your contribution to this world count.

You are here in this time and place on purpose,

so do your best to glorify God in all you do.

Shine the light back on Jesus.

Whatever work you do,
do it with all your heart.
Do it for the Lord AND NOT FOR MEN.
Colossians 3:23 NLV

ONE MORE THING

God loves you!

FOR I CAN DO EVERYTHING
through Christ who gives me strength.
Philippians
4:13 NLT
26